Baroque

Real Repertoire

Selected and edited by Christine Brown

Contents

Faber Music Bloomsbury House 74–77 Great Russell Street London WC1B 3DA
in association with
Trinity College London 89 Albert Embankment London SE1 7TP

EDITOR'S NOTE

The pieces in *Baroque Real Repertoire* have been selected to provide intermediate pianists with enjoyable music for private study or for performance in concerts, festivals and examinations. There is a wide choice as the pieces vary in technical difficulty, length, tempo, key, character and mood.

The fingering has been chosen with great care to produce good technical and musical results. The metronome marks, which are editorial, have been given as a guide but are not obligatory. The realisation of the ornaments is based on contemporary sources, frequently from the composer's own instructions. Editorial suggestions for dynamics and phrasing are shown either in brackets or, in a few places to aid clarity, by dotted lines.

The collection is not intended to be an urtext edition. As players progress they may wish to extend their knowledge of the music of this period by consulting urtext editions and making decisions for themselves. In this publication the editor has taken decisions with the intention of helping less experienced players to achieve a convincing performance in an authentic style.

I hope that these fine pieces will bring much pleasure to those who study and perform them and to their audiences.

Christine Brown

© 2005 by Faber Music Ltd and Trinity College London
First published in 2005 by Faber Music Ltd
in association with Trinity College London
Bloomsbury House 74–77 Great Russell Street London WC1B 3DA
Cover design by Sue Clarke
Original handwriting by Kathy Baxendale
Music processed by Jackie Leigh
Printed in England by Caligraving Ltd

ISBN10: 0-571-52333-1
EAN13: 978-0-571-52333-7

To buy Faber Music or Trinity publications or to find out about the full range of titles available please contact your local music retailer or Faber Music sales enquiries:

Faber Music Ltd, Burnt Mill, Elizabeth Way, Harlow CM20 2HX
Tel: +44 (0)1279 82 89 82   Fax: +44 (0)1279 82 89 83
sales@fabermusic.com   fabermusic.com   trinityguildhall.co.uk

THE BAROQUE PERIOD

The term Baroque when applied to music refers to works written during the period 1600 to 1750. The word has its origin in architecture which, like Baroque music, has a strong formal structure and often includes dramatic contrasts and much ornamentation.

THE KEYBOARD INSTRUMENTS

The pieces in this collection were written for the predecessors of the modern piano, namely the virginal, harpsichord, spinet and clavichord. The first three are similar in that the sound is produced by a string being plucked by a quill set in a small piece of wood called a jack. However, in the clavichord the string is struck by a tangent made of brass. These photographs of instruments in the Russell Collection help to clarify this:

Virginal by S. Keene (1668)
The virginal, rectangular in shape, has one set of strings which run parallel to the keyboard while the jacks, hidden by the jackrail, run at an angle.

Two-manual harpsichord by Jan Ruckers (1638)
In the harpsichord there may be two or three sets of strings, all of which run at right angles to the keyboard. Some harpsichords have two manuals, each with its own set of strings, so the player has the opportunity to vary the quantity and quality of tone produced.

Spinet by T. Hitchcock (c.1705)
The spinet has a triangular shape and one set of strings at an angle to the keyboard.

Clavichord by Dolmetsch (1896 copy modelled on C. G. Hoffmann, 1784)
In the clavichord one set of strings runs parallel to the keyboard. When a key is depressed the tangent strikes the string giving the player control over the volume and the possibility of prolonging the sound by continuing pressure on the key. However, the sound produced is very small so it is suitable only for domestic music making.

THE COMPOSERS AND THEIR PIECES

THOMAS AUGUSTINE ARNE (1710–1778), now well known as the composer of *Rule Britannia*, was much admired in his lifetime for his melodious music for the theatre and for his skill as a performer on the harpsichord. His set of *Eight Sonatas or Lessons for the Harpsichord* was published in London in 1756. He left details of registration to the performer, so there are no dynamic markings in the original. The attractive first movement of the *Sonata in A*, the seventh of the set, needs a firm rhythmic opening and care for the balance between the hands in the passage from bar 13 to bar 21. Here it is likely that two manuals would have been used to produce the effect of a melody and an accompaniment. Remember that *presto* in Arne's time was slower than it is today.

CARL PHILIPP EMANUEL BACH (1714–1788), perhaps the most talented of Johann Sebastian's musical sons, wrote over a hundred keyboard sonatas, many of which broke new ground in their treatment of form and technique, and was the author of an important treatise *Essay on the True Art of Playing Keyboard Instruments* (1753). The *Solo for the Cembalo* (an abbreviation of 'clavicembalo' meaning harpsichord) is one of the pieces in the *Notebook for Anna Magdalena Bach*. Johann Sebastian's first wife died in 1720 leaving him seven children and a year later he married the young singer Anna Magdalena who bore him thirteen more. The *Notebook*, beautifully bound, was a gift from her husband in 1725 and contained a selection of pieces written by members of the Bach family circle for her enjoyment. The *Solo* shows the young composer exploiting the dynamic possibilities of a two-manual instrument and moving away from his father's more contrapuntal style.

JOHANN SEBASTIAN BACH (1685–1750) is the overwhelmingly great figure of the Baroque period. He composed works of the highest quality in all the musical genres of his time except that of opera. Among his keyboard works are two volumes of preludes and fugues in each major and minor key, partitas, suites, fantasias, inventions, sinfonias and concertos. The set of fifteen inventions, written in a strict two-part contrapuntal style with one voice for each hand, was designed to teach basic keyboard technique and fingering in the keys up to four sharps and four flats. On the elaborate title page Bach claims that 'those desirous of learning' will be shown how to 'play clearly in two parts… and, above all, to arrive at a singing style in playing'. The pieces are ideally suited to Bach's favourite domestic instrument the clavichord, which was capable of the expressive variations of tone called for in the *Invention in A minor*. However, the *Echo from the French Overture*, sometimes called the *Partita in B minor*, was clearly intended for a two-manual harpsichord and Bach makes dramatic use of the two manuals by indicating with *forte* and *piano* markings the rapid changes required.

FRANÇOIS COUPERIN (1668–1733), known as Couperin the Great to distinguish him from his many musical relations, lived and worked in Paris. His compositions for the harpsichord were arranged in suite-like groups which he called Ordres. In addition to dance movements he included character pieces: portraits in sound of particular individuals. Famous as a virtuoso performer and a teacher he wrote *L'Art de toucher le clavecin* ('The Art of Playing the Harpsichord', 1716) which remains a valuable guide today. Incorporated in the treatise are eight *Preludes* of gradually increasing difficulty and an *Allemande* to illustrate his teaching methods. Couperin states that the *Allemande*, a German dance, must move lightly, so the fingers must be kept close to the keys and the chosen tempo must allow the ornaments to be clearly defined.

LOUIS-CLAUDE DAQUIN (1694–1772) was born and died in Paris. At the age of six he played the harpsichord in front of King Louis XIV and at twelve he played the organ in services at the Sainte-Chapelle. Later he became a distinguished performer on both instruments even beating Rameau in a competition for the post of organist at St Paul. During his lifetime he was renowned for his improvisations and now he is remembered for his compositions for the harpsichord. He wrote a book of *Noels* for keyboard and other instruments and four harpsichord *Suites* which include descriptive pieces such as *The Angry Winds* and *The Cuckoo*.

GEORGE FRIDERIC HANDEL (1685–1759) was equally famous in his lifetime as both a composer and keyboard player. Born in Saxony, he travelled round Europe in his youth then settled in England where he spent the rest of his life. He was buried in Westminster Abbey with much honour. Handel's compositions include operas, oratorios, keyboard and other instrumental music. His harpsichord music includes many suites as well as other miscellaneous pieces such as sets of variations and fugues. The sarabande, one of the most popular dances of the Baroque period was almost always to be found in a suite along with an allemande, a courante and a gigue. Spanish in origin, the sarabande is in triple time and often has a serious or melancholy character. Handel lengthens the *Sarabande* from his *Suite in D minor* by adding two beautiful variations. The *Allegro* from the *Suite in G major* is placed between the *Allemande* and the *Courante* where it serves an expressive rather than a virtuoso purpose.

PIETRO DOMENICO PARADIES (1707–1791) was born in Naples and died in Venice, although he spent many years working as a performer, composer and teacher in London. He was a fine harpsichordist and is best remembered for his twelve harpsichord sonatas (1754), the well-known *Toccata* being the second movement of the sixth *Sonata*. A toccata has no particular form but is a piece designed to show off the performer's touch. The *Toccata in A* requires sparkling finger work and clear articulation to make its effect.

HENRY PURCELL (1659–1695) is now regarded as one of the greatest of English composers. From early childhood he was a chorister of the Chapel Royal and received an excellent musical education. At the age of only twenty-two he was appointed Organist of Westminster Abbey and after his early death was interred beneath the organ. Among his instrumental works are suites for the harpsichord and numerous attractive miscellaneous pieces. The contrapuntal *Prelude* from the fifth *Suite* requires clear articulation and careful attention to the timing of the ornaments so that they do not impede the flow of the semiquavers. The composer's instructions for the correct realisation of the ornaments can be found in the 'Rules for Graces' in his *A Choice Collection of Lessons for the Harpsichord or Spinet* (1696). Purcell was renowned as a master of the ground, a short bass line repeated with varied parts above it. *A New Ground*, his own arrangement of one of his songs, would have sounded best on a two-manual harpsichord. The three-bar ground and the syncopated figure would have been played on one manual and the song melody on the other.

JEAN PHILIPPE RAMEAU (1683–1764) was called by his friend Voltaire 'le premier musicien de France'. Famous as an organist, a theorist, a composer and a teacher of the harpsichord, he published suites of pieces for the 'clavecin' in 1706 and 1724. Many of the pieces were based on dances: the allemande, courante, menuet, gavotte and gigue; while others, known as genre pieces, had an extra-musical derivation such as the imitation of natural sounds. The title *Le rappel des oiseaux* is not easy to translate, but it suggests birds gathering together. Their cheerful calls are heard clearly in the 'pincé' (pinched) ornaments which depict their chirping.

DOMENICO SCARLATTI (1685–1757), son of the famous opera composer Alessandro, was born in Naples. His musical career in Italy included serving as musical director at St. Peter's in Rome. Later he left Italy to travel in England and Portugal, where he became music teacher to the members of the royal family. The young Infanta Maria Barbara was exceptionally talented and he went with her entourage to Spain when she married. There he wrote most of his over five hundred amazingly varied and original sonatas for the harpsichord. The sonata in the Baroque era was a one-movement piece in binary form, but Scarlatti sometimes seemed to anticipate the sonata form of the Classical age. The nickname 'Pastorale' was given to the *Sonata in D minor* in Tausig's nineteenth-century piano arrangement and suggests the serene mood of this beautiful piece. The *Sonata in D major*, marked to be played in the time or style of a dance, is lively and energetic making considerable technical demands on the performer. There are no dynamics in Scarlatti's original manuscripts and very few marks of phrasing. The editorial dynamics suggest the broad contrasts possible on a two-manual harpsichord. K stands for the Kirkpatrick catalogue number.

PRESTO

First movement *from* Sonata in A

Thomas Augustine Arne
(1710–1778)

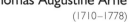

There are no phrasing or expression marks in the original manuscript. Play the semiquavers smoothly and the quavers detached or slurred as suggested in the left hand of bar 4.

INVENTION IN A MINOR

BWV784

Johann Sebastian Bach
(1685–1750)

Phrase as the editor suggests in the first bar i.e. play the quavers lightly detached and the semiquavers smoothly.

ECHO

from the French Overture in B minor, BWV831

Johann Sebastian Bach
(1685–1750)

The dynamic markings *forte* and *piano* without brackets are Bach's own and suitable for a two-manual harpsichord.
The editor has added similar markings as appropriate.

SOLO FOR THE CEMBALO

BWV Anh. 129

Carl Philipp Emanuel Bach
(1714–1788)

The dynamics are editorial, suggesting the registration on a two-manual harpsichord.

ALLEMANDE IN D MINOR

from L'Art de toucher le clavecin

François Couperin
(1668–1733)

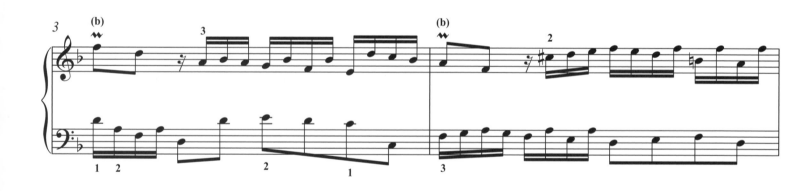

The slurs in bars 2, 5, 11 and 12 are original. Ornaments a, d and e may be omitted.

LE COUCOU

Rondeau

Louis-Claude Daquin
(1694–1772)

Keep the semiquavers light throughout and articulate the cuckoo calls (falling minor thirds) clearly by playing the quaver *staccato* each time.

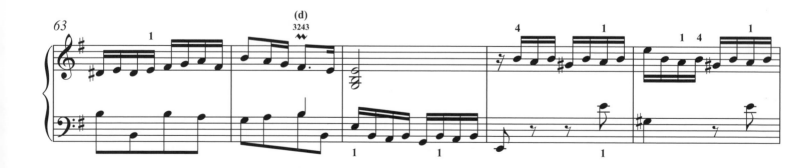

22

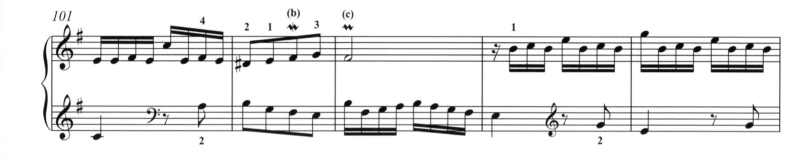

This page is blank to help with page turns

ALLEGRO

from Suite No.8 in G

George Frideric Handel
(1685–1759)

Play smoothly and expressively, holding notes for their full value. The cadential chords may be arpeggiated.

SARABANDE

from Suite in D minor

George Frideric Handel
(1685–1759)

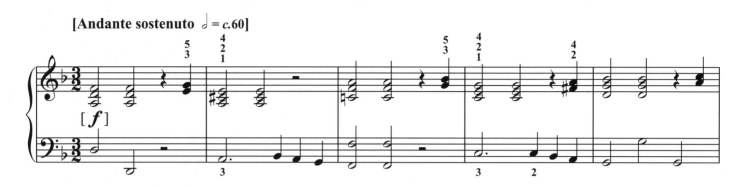

Variation I

The dynamics are editorial and may be varied if desired.

Variation 2

TOCCATA IN A MAJOR

from Sonata No.6

Pietro Domenico Paradies
(1707–1791)

* There are no dynamics or phrase-marks in the original. Play the semiquavers smoothly and the quavers detached or slurred in pairs as suggested on the first line.

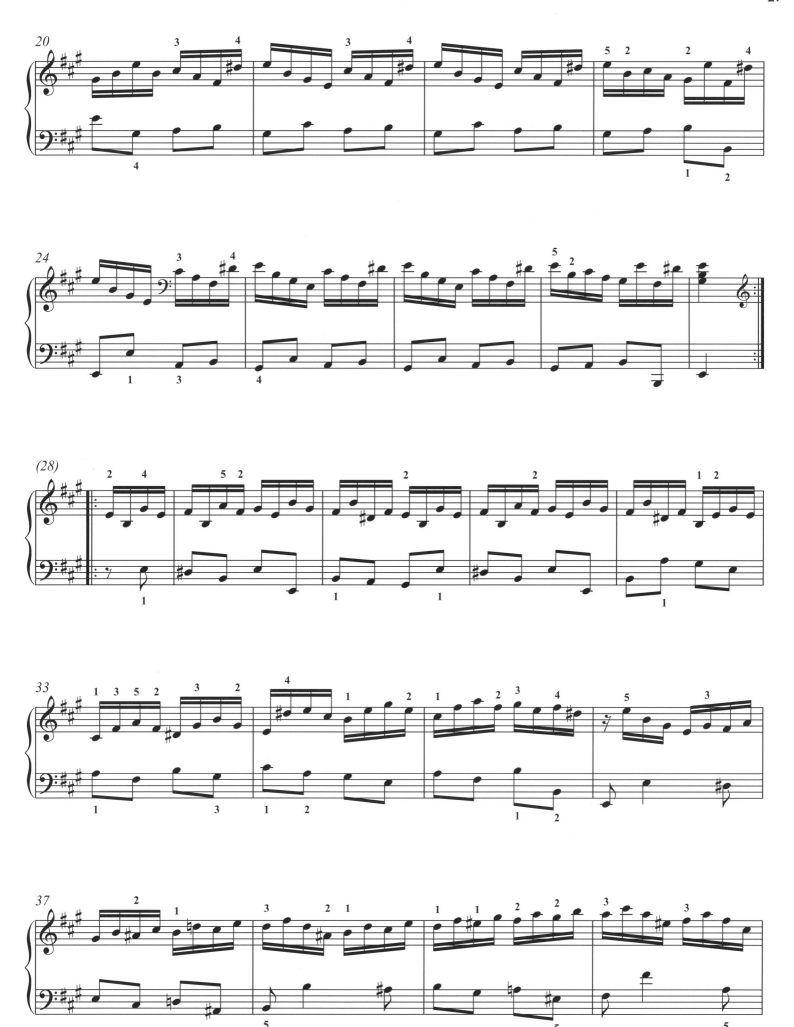

PRELUDE

from Suite No.5 in C, Z666

Henry Purcell
(1659–1695)

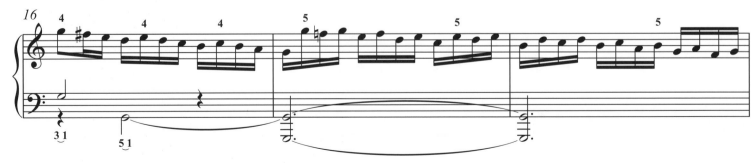

* Phrase as the editor suggests in the first bar i.e. play the quavers detached and the semiquavers smoothly.

LE RAPPEL DES OISEAUX

Jean Philippe Rameau
(1683–1764)

Play lightly and articulate the bird calls clearly. Detach each semiquaver before a tied note.

A NEW GROUND IN E MINOR

'Here the Deities Approve'
from Welcome to All the Pleasures, Z.T682

Henry Purcell
(1659–1695)

The melody which starts in bar 3 should sing out above the ground bass and the middle voice as if on a two-manual harpsichord.

SONATA IN D

K430

Domenico Scarlatti
(1685–1757)

* The phrasing suggested in bars 1– 4 and 9–12 may be used throughout. The dynamics are editorial,
suggesting the registration on a two-manual harpsichord.

SONATA IN D MINOR

'Pastorale', K9

Domenico Scarlatti
(1685–1757)

In the opening bars, and in similar places, the left hand should play more softly than the right hand, as if on a two-manual harpsichord. The trills could be in demisemiquavers if preferred. Keep the scale passages light.

44

SONATA IN C

K159

Domenico Scarlatti
(1685–1757)

The dynamics are editorial, suggesting the registration on a two-manual harpsichord.